# THE
# HOLIDAYS
## COOKBOOK

### Menus, Recipes, and Wine Selections for Holiday Entertaining

**Virginia and Robert Hoffman**

The Crossing Press
Freedom, California

ISBN 0-89594-843-5

# CONTENTS

# INTRODUCTION

All the menus indicate the number of servings for the whole meal. If you are entertaining a different number of guests, just change the amounts of the ingredients. The menus are meant as suggestions; recipes may be moved from one menu to another.

Many of these recipes can be prepared ahead. We have done this so you can enjoy holiday entertaining with your family and guests instead of working in the kitchen until the last minute.

We have suggested wines to accompany the menus in this book. The selections are based upon our own preferences and those of others in the food and wine field. But everyone's taste is different! If you prefer a wine other than the ones we have suggested, enjoy it.

We hope that you have as much pleasure in using this cookbook as we did in writing it.

*Virginia and Robert Hoffman*
*Santa Rosa, California*

# TRADITIONAL THANKSGIVING DINNER

### (FOR EIGHT)

*Oysters on the Half Shell*
*Creamed Corn Soup*
*Celery ~ Radishes ~ Olives*
*Roast Turkey with Chestnut Stuffing and Giblet Gravy*
*Cranberry Sauce ~ Spiced Apples*
*Mashed Potatoes ~ Brussels Sprouts*
*Onions in Cream*
*Pumpkin Pie ~ Mincemeat Pie ~ Vanilla Ice Cream*
*Assorted Nuts ~ Fruit ~ Chocolate Mints ~ Coffee*

## We suggest

- *With the oysters—champagne or a California sparkling wine.*
- *With the main course—an earthy pinot noir or spicy Gewürztraminer.*
- *With coffee and dessert—a fine Cognac or brandy.*

# OYSTERS ON THE HALF SHELL

You will need 4 to 6 fresh oysters per person. Have the store halve the oysters and pack them with ice for the trip home. Keep very cold until ready to serve. Serve on a bed of rock salt, with lemon wedges and hot sauce. (The rock salt will keep the oysters from tipping.)

Bottled oysters can be used instead of fresh oysters. Serve them in small glass bowls (such as soup bowls) embedded in ice, with lemon wedges and hot sauce on the side.

# CREAMED CORN SOUP

3 tablespoons butter
1 medium onion, thinly sliced
1/2 cup green pepper, finely diced
2 potatoes, thinly sliced
2 cups boiling water
2 cups milk, divided
1 tablespoon flour
1/2 bay leaf
1 can (19 ounces) of cream-style corn
Salt and pepper to taste

Heat butter in saucepan, add onion and green pepper and cook over low heat 3 minutes, stirring frequently. Add potatoes and water; bring to a boil. Lower heat, cover and boil until potatoes are tender.

Mix 1/3 cup of the milk with the flour. Add to boiling mixture. Add the remaining ingredients. Simmer 15 minutes, stirring frequently. Remove bay leaf. Place the soup in a blender and whip until creamy. Serve hot or cold. Salt and pepper to taste.

# Roast Turkey

1 whole turkey, 12 to 14 pounds
Salt and pepper to taste

Preheat oven to 350 degrees. Set aside neck and giblets for gravy.

Wash turkey with cold water, dry, and rub salt and pepper into body cavities. Spoon the stuffing (recipe follows) into body cavities. Do not pack tightly. Close skin with skewers or twine and tie drumsticks together.

Place the turkey on a rack in a roasting pan, uncovered, in oven for 20 minutes per pound. Test after three hours for doneness with a fork to see if juices run clear or with a thermometer for an internal temperature of 175 to 180 degrees.

If the turkey gets too dark, place an aluminum foil "tent" over the breast.

Remove from oven, place on platter, and allow the turkey to stand for 20 minutes before carving.

# Chestnut Stuffing

2 pounds chestnuts
2 cups butter
2 cups onions, finely minced
2 cups celery, finely minced
10 cups dry bread crumbs
1 teaspoon dried thyme
1 teaspoon dried marjoram
1 teaspoon dried savory
1 teaspoon dried rosemary
Salt to taste

With a sharp paring knife cut a cross on the flat side of each chestnut. Simmer, covered with water, in a saucepan for 5 minutes. Drain. While hot, remove the shells and inner brown skins. Cover with fresh water and boil for 20 to 30 minutes until tender. Drain; chop coarsely.

Melt the butter in saucepan, add onions and celery; cook until limp. Add bread crumbs, and spices. Mix thoroughly. Add chestnuts; mix thoroughly. Salt to taste.

After the turkey is stuffed, any extra stuffing can be baked in a covered casserole in the oven with the turkey for the last hour.

# GIBLET GRAVY

Neck and giblets of turkey
4 cups boiling water
2 cups white wine
4 whole peppercorns
1 sprig parsley
1 medium onion
2 whole cloves
1 carrot
5 tablespoons flour
Salt and pepper to taste

Cover neck and giblets in a saucepan with the boiling water and all ingredients except the flour. Boil for 1 minute. Skim residue, cover, and lower heat to simmer contents for 1 hour. Strain the broth to remove the spices, onion, and carrot. Save the neck and giblets. Remove meat from neck, and mince giblets and neck meat. Reserve.

Pour off all but 6 tablespoons of the fat from the drippings in the turkey pan. Place roasting pan over low heat and stir in the flour. Cook until thickened and bubbling. Add the broth, stirring. Add chopped neck meat and giblets just before serving. Salt and pepper to taste.

# CRANBERRY SAUCE

2 pounds fresh cranberries
2 cups water
2 cups brown sugar
1 cup chopped walnuts
1 cup raisins

Cook the cranberries in the water with the brown sugar until they pop open. Reduce the heat to a simmer, and add the walnuts and raisins. Simmer for 10 to 15 minutes; refrigerate. This sauce may be made up to a week in advance.

# SPICED APPLES

2 pounds tart cooking apples
2 cups sugar
1 pint wine vinegar
1 stick cinnamon
1/2 teaspoon whole cloves

Pare, core, and slice apples horizontally, 1/2 inch thick, and then cut the slices into quarters. Place all ingredients in a saucepan, bring to a boil, and cook for 5 minutes. Reduce to a simmer, and cook until tender. The apples should remain in the syrup until ready to serve. This dish may be made up to a week ahead.

# Mashed Potatoes

4 pounds potatoes
2 tablespoons butter
3/4 cup warm milk
Salt and pepper to taste

Peel and quarter potatoes, removing any eyes, dark areas, or other blemishes. Boil for 20 to 25 minutes until tender; drain. Mash with mixer at low speed or with a potato masher until lumps are completely gone. Add the butter as you mash. Continue mashing, and add the milk slowly until the desired consistency is reached. (You may need more or less milk than the amount listed.) Add salt and pepper to taste.

# Brussels Sprouts

1 1/2 pounds Brussels sprouts
1 medium yellow onion, peeled and
    sliced
1/4 cup balsamic vinegar
3 tablespoons butter, divided
Salt and pepper to taste

Cut off the stems and remove any limp leaves from the Brussels sprouts. Blanch them in boiling water for 5 minutes. Drain and rinse the sprouts with cold water to stop the cooking process.

Heat a large frying pan and add 1 tablespoon of the butter. When the butter is melted, add the onions and sauté until they are translucent. Add the sprouts. Sauté for a few minutes until they are cooked, but still firm. Add the vinegar and toss to ensure all sprouts are thoroughly coated. Add the remaining butter and salt and pepper to taste.

# ONIONS IN CREAM

3 pounds pearl onions or very small
   yellow onions
2 cups chicken broth
2 tablespoons butter
6 tablespoons flour
1/3 cup dry sherry
1 cup half-and-half
1/4 teaspoon ground nutmeg
1 tablespoon chopped fresh parsley

Preheat oven to 375 degrees.

Trim and peel onions, and then place them in a saucepan. Add the chicken broth and bring to a boil. Cover and simmer for 10 minutes, or until just tender. Strain, remove the onions, and put them aside. Continue simmering the stock.

Melt the butter in a small frying pan, and add flour. Cook together for a few minutes, but do not allow them to get brown. Add this to the stock, and stir until thickened and smooth. Stir in the sherry and half-and-half. Simmer for 2 minutes more. Add nutmeg and parsley.

Combine the onions with the sauce in a casserole and bake for 40 to 45 minutes until the casserole is bubbling. Brown, if you wish, under the broiler.

# PUMPKIN PIE

1 can (16 ounces) of pumpkin
3/4 cup sugar
1 teaspoon ground cinnamon
1/2 teaspoon ground ginger
1/2 teaspoon ground nutmeg
1/2 teaspoon salt
3 eggs
2/3 cup (15-ounce can) evaporated milk
1/2 cup milk
Pastry for single crust pie

Preheat oven to 375 degrees. In a large bowl, combine pumpkin, sugar, all spices, salt, and the eggs. Lightly beat eggs into the mixture with a fork. Add the milk and evaporated milk; mix thoroughly.

Line a 9-inch pie plate with the pastry, trim, and fill with the pumpkin mixture. Cover rim of pie with foil. Bake for 25 minutes, remove foil, and return to oven for 25 minutes or until knife inserted in the center comes out clean. Cool. Cover and chill to serve. Sweetened whipped cream is a nice way to gild this lily.

# MINCEMEAT PIE

1/2 cup raisins
1/4 cup brandy
2 cups mincemeat
1/2 cup orange marmalade
2 tablespoons flour
1 tablespoon lemon juice
1/4 teaspoon ground nutmeg
Pastry for a double crust pie

Preheat oven to 425 degrees.

Soak the raisins in the brandy for at least an hour. Combine all ingredients except pastry; mix thoroughly. Line a 9-inch pie plate with pastry, fill, and place remaining pastry over all. Crimp top over bottom and trim excess. Perforate top, and if desired, sprinkle with milk and sugar to achieve more browning.

Bake for 25 minutes. Serve warm. Ice cream is good with this.

# New England Thanksgiving Dinner

### (For Eight)

*Carrot Bisque*
*Roast Turkey with Molasses Glaze*
*Giblet Gravy ~ Corn Bread–Sage Dressing*
*Mashed Parsnip Potatoes ~ Red Pepper Succotash*
*Cranberry Relish with Pears and Apples*
*Classic New England Cider Pie*
*Coffee ~ Tea*

## We suggest
- *With the main course—an earthy pinot noir or a ripe red burgundy.*
  *You could also serve a soft, light merlot.*
- *With dessert—a tawny port or a fine sherry.*

# CARROT BISQUE

1/4 cup plus 2 tablespoons butter
2 pounds carrots, peeled and sliced thin
2 large onions, peeled and chopped
1 tablespoon peeled, minced fresh ginger
2 teaspoons grated orange peel
1/2 teaspoon ground coriander
5 cups chicken broth, divided
1 cup half-and-half
Salt and pepper to taste
1/2 cup minced fresh parsley

Melt butter in heavy large saucepan over medium heat. Add carrots and onions. Cover saucepan and cook until vegetables begin to soften, stirring occasionally, about 15 minutes. Mix in ginger, orange peel, and coriander. Add 2 cups of the broth.

Reduce heat to medium low. Cover pan and simmer until carrots are very tender, about 30 minutes.

Purée the soup in batches in a blender. Add the remaining 3 cups broth and the half-and-half to the soup. Add salt and pepper to taste.

Serve hot with a sprinkle of parsley over each bowl.

# ROAST TURKEY WITH MOLASSES GLAZE

1 whole turkey, 15 pounds
Salt and pepper to taste
Poultry seasoning, to taste
1 onion
3 tablespoons butter, melted, divided
2 cups plus 2 tablespoons chicken stock, divided
1 tablespoon dark molasses
1 teaspoon red wine vinegar
Fresh sage sprigs (optional)

Preheat oven to 350 degrees. (Set aside neck and giblets. You can use these for the gravy.)

Rinse turkey inside and out. Dry thoroughly. Discard any pieces of fat in neck or main cavity. Season neck cavity with salt and pepper. Fold neck skin over and secure to body with skewer. Season main body cavity with salt, pepper, and poultry seasoning. Place onion in cavity. Sew or skewer main cavity closed. Tuck wings under turkey body. Tie legs together.

Place turkey, breast side up, on rack in large roasting pan. Brush 2 tablespoons of the melted butter over turkey. Pour 1/2 cup of the stock or broth into pan.

Roast turkey 2 1/2 hours, basting with pan juices and adding 1/2 cup chicken stock to pan about every 45 minutes. Combine remaining 1 tablespoon melted butter with molasses and vinegar. Brush glaze over turkey.

Roast turkey about 30 minutes longer, until meat thermometer inserted into thickest part of thigh registers 175 degrees.

Transfer turkey to platter and tent with foil. Let stand 20 to 30 minutes.

Garnish turkey with fresh sage sprigs, if desired.

# Giblet Gravy

Turkey pan juices
6 tablespoons turkey fat
7 tablespoons flour
5 cups giblet broth (recipe follows) or
    canned low-salt chicken broth
1/3 cup dry sherry
Salt and pepper to taste

Pour turkey juices from roasting pan into a bowl. Degrease juices in the bowl, reserving 6 tablespoons fat. Pour reserved fat back into the roasting pan. Place the pan over medium heat. Add the flour to the roasting pan and whisk until beginning to brown, about 3 minutes.

Gradually whisk in giblet broth, degreased pan juices, and sherry. Simmer until the gravy thickens, whisking and scraping bottom of the pan, about 10 minutes. Mix in giblets and neck meat reserved from giblet broth. Season gravy to taste with salt and pepper.

Transfer gravy to sauceboat or serving dish.

# Giblet Broth

6 cups low-salt chicken broth
Turkey neck and giblets
1 small onion, peeled and halved
2 celery stalks with tops, coarsely
    chopped
1 teaspoon chopped fresh sage or
    1/2 teaspoon crumbled dried sage
Pinch of pepper

Combine all ingredients except turkey liver in a heavy large saucepan and bring to boil. Reduce heat, cover partially, and simmer 1 1/2 hours. Rinse liver and add to broth.

Simmer until liver is cooked through, about 10 minutes. Remove giblets and reserve. Strain broth, discarding vegetables. Carefully remove the meat from the neck. Finely chop giblets and neck meat and reserve for gravy.

Cover and chill broth and chopped meats separately until ready to use.

# CORN BREAD–SAGE DRESSING

5 cups coarse corn bread crumbs
7 tablespoons butter
3 large celery stalks, chopped
2 medium onions, peeled and chopped
3 tablespoons chopped fresh sage or
   1 tablespoon dried, crumbled sage
Salt and pepper to taste
4 cups 1/2-inch cubes white bread
3/4 cup chicken stock or canned low-salt
   broth
1 egg, beaten to blend

Preheat oven to 350 degrees. Butter one large or two medium casserole dishes.

Crumble the corn bread coarsely onto a large cookie sheet. Let stand uncovered at room temperature overnight to dry.

Melt butter in a heavy large skillet over medium heat. Add celery and onions and fry until tender, stirring frequently, about 12 minutes. Transfer mixture to a large bowl. Mix in sage, salt, and pepper. (This stage can be prepared one day ahead. Cover and refrigerate.) Add corn bread crumbs and bread cubes to vegetables. Combine the stock and egg in a small bowl. Stir into dressing. Add salt and pepper to taste.

Bake for 1 hour. It can bake during the last 30 minutes while the turkey is browning in the oven and then while the turkey is sitting before it is carved. Serve the dressing hot.

# MASHED PARSNIP POTATOES

4 pounds russet potatoes, peeled
1 1/2 pounds parsnips, peeled
Water to cover
1/2 cup (1 stick) butter
2 green onions, chopped
1 1/2 cups milk
Minced fresh parsley for garnish

Cut the potatoes and parsnips into 1 1/2-inch pieces. Place in a saucepan, cover with water and boil until very tender, about 20 minutes. Drain well.

Melt the butter in the same pot over low heat. Add onions and sauté 1 minute. Add milk and bring just to simmer. Add potatoes and parsnips to pot; mash until smooth. Season with salt and pepper.

Serve hot, garnished with chopped parsley.

# RED PEPPER SUCCOTASH

6 cups frozen lima beans
Water to cover
6 cups frozen corn kernels
1 1/2 cups finely chopped red bell pepper
   (about 1 1/2 peppers)
3 tablespoons butter
1 cup plus 2 tablespoons cream
1/2 teaspoon sugar
Salt and pepper to taste
Minced fresh parsley for garnish

Cook lima beans for about 6 minutes covered with water until almost tender. Add corn and bring to a simmer. Add red pepper and cook 2 minutes. Drain well.

Return the vegetables to the same saucepan. Add butter and toss to coat. Add cream and cook over medium heat until sauce thickens, stirring occasionally, for about 10 minutes. Add sugar. Season with salt and pepper to taste. Serve hot, sprinkled with parsley.

# CRANBERRY RELISH WITH PEARS AND APPLES

3 tart apples, such as Granny Smith or
 pippin, peeled, cored, and diced
2 ripe pears, peeled, cored, and diced
2 pounds fresh cranberries
2 cups sugar
1 cup golden raisins
1 cup freshly squeezed orange juice
2 tablespoons grated orange rind
2 teaspoons ground cinnamon
1/4 teaspoon ground nutmeg
1/2 cup brandy

Mix together all the ingredients except the brandy in a saucepan. Bring to a boil, reduce the heat and simmer, uncovered, for 45 minutes, until thick. Stir in the brandy, let cool to room temperature and refrigerate, covered, until serving time.

# CLASSIC NEW ENGLAND CIDER PIE

2 1/2 cups apple cider
2 1/2 pounds tart apples (about 6) peeled, cored, sliced thinly
1 pound golden delicious apples (about 2) peeled, cored, sliced thinly
1 cup sugar
1/4 cup flour
1/2 teaspoon ground cinnamon
1/4 teaspoon ground mace
1/4 teaspoon salt
4 teaspoons fresh lemon juice
3 tablespoons butter, cut into small pieces
Pastry for a double crust pie

Boil cider for about 25 minutes in heavy small saucepan until reduced to 2/3 cup. Cool.

Position rack in lowest third of oven and preheat the oven to 425 degrees. Combine all apples, sugar, flour, cinnamon, mace, and salt in a large bowl. Add reduced cider and lemon juice and toss well.

Roll out the pie crust on a lightly floured surface to a 14-inch round. Transfer to a 10-inch pie plate. Gently press into place. Trim edges of crust, leaving 1/2-inch overhang. Spoon apples into crust-lined pan, mounding in center. Dot with butter. Roll out the remaining dough to a 13-inch round and gently place over pie. Trim edges, leaving 3/4-inch overhang. Fold overhang of top crust under edge of bottom crust. Pinch together to seal. Crimp edges to make decorative border. Cut slashes in top crust to allow steam to escape.

Bake pie 25 minutes, then reduce oven temperature to 350 degrees. Continue baking until filling bubbles, about 50 minutes longer. Cover edges with foil if browning too quickly. Cool. Serve pie warm or at room temperature.

# SOUTHERN THANKSGIVING DINNER

### (FOR EIGHT)

*Watercress Soup*
*Roast Turkey with Oyster Stuffing*
*Country Green Beans ~ Corn Pudding*
*Sweet Potato Apricot Bake*
*Cheddar Cheese Biscuits ~ Cranberry-Ginger Chutney*
*Pumpkin Pie*
*Coffee ~ Tea*

## We suggest
- *With the main course—a dry chenin blanc to start, followed by a floral Riesling, perhaps a Spatlese, or a Grand Cru white.*
- *With dessert—a cremant (slightly sweet) champagne or sparkling Malvasia.*

# WATERCRESS SOUP

1/2 pound butter or margarine
2 medium onions, peeled and chopped
4 bunches watercress
1/2 cup flour
4 cups low salt chicken broth
2 cups milk
Salt and pepper to taste

Melt butter in a saucepan, add onion and cook gently for 10 minutes until soft. Set aside.

Wash and trim the watercress, removing most of the stems, but leaving a few. Chop the few stems and leaves coarsely. Add the watercress to the onions. Cover the pan, and cook gently for 4 minutes.

Add the flour and cook gently, stirring, for 2 minutes. Remove from heat and gradually add broth and milk. Bring to a boil, then simmer for 4 minutes. Add salt and pepper to taste.

Purée in a blender or food processor. This soup may be prepared a day or two ahead and gently reheated when ready to serve.

# Roast Turkey with Oyster Stuffing

*The Stuffing:*

1 loaf white bread (1 pound), sliced
2 cups finely chopped celery
   (7 to 8 stalks)
2 cups minced onion
3/4 cup butter or margarine (1 1/2 sticks)
1/2 cup milk
24 ounces (3 containers) fresh, frozen, or
   canned oysters
1 teaspoon lemon juice
1/4 teaspoon ground nutmeg
3/4 teaspoon poultry seasoning
Salt and pepper to taste

1 whole turkey, 12 to 14 pounds
Salt and pepper to taste

Dry bread slices overnight in open air or on a rack in a 250 degree oven for 1 to 1 1/4 hours.

In a skillet, sauté celery and onion in butter until tender. Set aside.

Warm milk over low heat in small saucepan. Tear bread into 1/2-inch pieces, making about 11 cups; place in a large mixing bowl. Sprinkle warm milk over the bread, tossing lightly. Add onion and celery along with the melted butter and the oysters to the bread mixture; toss to mix well. Sprinkle with lemon juice, nutmeg, poultry seasoning, salt and pepper to taste; mix thoroughly.

Preheat oven to 325 degrees.

Rinse turkey; pat dry. Rub salt and pepper into neck and body cavities. Lightly spoon dressing into neck cavity; close with skewer. Fill body cavity. Secure drumsticks lightly with a string. Roast uncovered on roasting rack for 20 to 22 minutes per pound or to an internal temperature of 170 to 180 degrees.

Any remaining dressing may be baked in a covered casserole along with the turkey during the last hour of roasting. Uncover the dressing during the final 10 minutes of cooking. Let the turkey stand at least 20 minutes before carving.

# COUNTRY GREEN BEANS

2 pounds fresh green beans, trimmed
Boiling water to cover
1/2 pound 1/4-inch-thick sliced country
   ham, cut into 2-inch strips
1 cup chopped onion
1/3 cup cider or distilled white vinegar
1 tablespoon sugar
Salt and pepper to taste

Put green beans in a large pot of boiling water. Cook about 6 minutes until beans are tender. Drain the beans and rinse under cold water. Pat dry and reserve.

Cook ham in a large skillet over medium heat until brown and crisp. Drain on paper towels. Pour off all but 1 tablespoon drippings.

Add the onion to the skillet; sauté for 3 to 5 minutes or until tender. Add the ham, then the cider or vinegar, sugar, salt and pepper. Cook, stirring, until mixture is hot and bubbly. Add cooked beans; toss to coat. Serve hot.

# CORN PUDDING

3 tablespoons butter
1 1/2 medium onions, peeled and chopped
1/4 cup flour
3 eggs
4 cups fresh corn kernels, or frozen corn
   kernels, thawed
1 1/2 cups milk
Salt and pepper to taste

Position rack in center of oven and preheat to 350 degrees. Butter two 6-cup casserole dishes. Set aside.

Melt butter in a large skillet over medium heat. Add onions and sauté until soft, about 12 minutes. Mix in flour and stir 4 minutes. Put in a bowl and cool.

Add eggs to onion mixture. Whisk to blend. Mix in corn, milk, salt, and pepper.

Divide batter evenly between prepared dishes. Bake until knife inserted into the center of each comes out clean, about 1 hour.

# Sweet Potato Apricot Bake

2 1/4 pounds (about 6) medium yams, or sweet potatoes cooked, drained, and pared
1/4 cup plus 2 tablespoons light brown sugar, divided
1 tablespoon flour
1/2 teaspoon ground cinnamon
1/8 teaspoon salt
1 1/2 cups orange juice
2 tablespoons butter
1 tablespoon orange liqueur (optional)
2 to 3 teaspoons grated orange rind
1 cup dried apricots, halved or quartered
1/4 cup golden raisins
1 cup pecans, chopped

Preheat oven to 350 degrees.

Cut the yams or sweet potatoes in half lengthwise; place in a single layer in a 2-quart shallow baking dish.

Combine 1/4 cup of the brown sugar, and the flour, cinnamon, and salt in a medium saucepan. Mix well. Gradually stir in the orange juice until the mixture is well blended and smooth. Bring the mixture to boiling over medium heat; cook, stirring constantly for 1 minute.

Remove from the heat; stir in the butter until melted. Add the orange liqueur, if using, the orange rind, apricots, and raisins. Pour the mixture over the potatoes in the baking dish. Sprinkle with the pecans and the remaining 2 tablespoons brown sugar.

Bake for 30 minutes or until hot and bubbly.

# CHEDDAR CHEESE BISCUITS

1 1/4 cups flour
1 1/2 teaspoons baking powder
1/2 teaspoon salt
2 tablespoons solid vegetable shortening
3 tablespoons shredded cheddar cheese
1/2 cup buttermilk
1/4 cup chopped green onions

Preheat oven to 425 degrees. Lightly butter one large cookie sheet.

Combine flour, baking powder, and salt in bowl. Add shortening and cut in until mixture resembles coarse meal. Stir in cheese. Add buttermilk and onions, and mix well. Turn out dough onto lightly floured surface and roll out to thickness of 1/4 inch.

Cut out biscuits using a 1 1/4-inch round biscuit cutter. Transfer biscuits to cookie sheet.

Bake until puffed and light golden, about 15 minutes. Serve warm. The biscuits can be prepared ahead and reheated before serving.

# CRANBERRY-GINGER CHUTNEY

1 1/4 cups fresh cranberries
16 dried apricots, quartered
3/4 cup light brown sugar
1/4 cup dried currants
2 tablespoons peeled, minced fresh ginger
2 tablespoons cranberry juice cocktail
3/4 teaspoon ground cinnamon
1/4 teaspoon cayenne

Combine all ingredients in heavy medium saucepan. Cook over medium heat, stirring to dissolve sugar. Increase heat to high and boil 3 minutes. Transfer to a bowl. Cool. This chutney can be prepared up to one week ahead of time. Refrigerate in an airtight container.

# Pumpkin Pie

2 eggs, slightly beaten
3/4 cup sugar
1 1/2 teaspoons ground cinnamon
1/2 teaspoon ground nutmeg
1/2 teaspoon ground ginger
1/4 teaspoon ground allspice
1/4 teaspoon ground cloves
1/2 teaspoon salt
1 can (1 pound) pumpkin
3 tablespoons molasses
2 cans (6 ounces each) evaporated milk
1 egg white, unbeaten
1/4 cup finely chopped pecans
8 whole pecan halves
Pastry for a single crust pie
Whipped cream (optional)

Preheat oven to 400 degrees.

To make the filling, combine the eggs, sugar, spices, salt, pumpkin, molasses, and evaporated milk in a large bowl. Combine with a wooden spoon until mixture is smooth.

Lightly brush pie shell with egg white. Sprinkle chopped pecans in bottom of pie shell. Fill with pumpkin mixture. Gently arrange pecan halves on filling around edge of pie.

Bake 55 to 60 minutes or until tip of sharp knife inserted in center comes out clean. Let cool on wire rack. Serve garnished with whipped cream, if using.

# New England Christmas Dinner

### (For Eight)

*Oysters on the Half Shell*
*Pumpkin Soup*
*Roast Beef with Glazed Onions and Gravy*
*Celeried Mashed Potatoes*
*Broccoli with Hazelnuts*
*Rolls*
*Chocolate Butterscotch Pie*
*Coffee ~ Tea*

**We suggest**
- *With the first courses—a buttery chardonnay.*
- *With the beef—an eight- to ten-year-old cabernet sauvignon or Bordeaux.*
- *To finish—a vintage port or Madeira.*

# Oysters on the Half Shell

You will need 4 or 6 fresh oysters per person. Have the store halve the oysters and pack them with ice for the trip home. Keep oysters very cold until ready to serve. Serve on a bed of rock salt, with a lemon cut into eighths, and hot sauce. (The salt serves to keep the oysters from tipping.)

Bottled oysters can be used instead of fresh ones. Serve them in small glass bowls (such as soup bowls) embedded in ice, with lemon wedges and hot sauce.

# Pumpkin Soup

1 tablespoon vegetable oil
2 small onions, peeled and finely minced
3 cups chicken broth
1 can (16 ounces) pumpkin
1 cup evaporated skim milk
1/4 teaspoon ginger curry seasoning
1/4 teaspoon ground nutmeg
1/4 teaspoon cayenne
1/4 teaspoon ground allspice
1/4 teaspoon ground cinnamon
Chopped chives for garnish

Heat a medium saucepan. When the pan is hot, add oil and heat for an additional minute.

Add the onions and sauté for about 4 to 5 minutes until translucent. Add the chicken broth and pumpkin. Mix thoroughly. Reduce heat and simmer for 15 minutes. Add evaporated milk and seasonings; simmer for an additional 5 minutes. Serve hot, garnished with chopped chives.

# ROAST BEEF WITH GLAZED ONIONS AND GRAVY

2 large onions, peeled and sliced thin
1 can (14 to 16 ounces) whole tomatoes, crushed
1 1/2 tablespoons vegetable oil
Salt and pepper to taste
4-pound boneless tied rib roast (at room temperature)
2 tablespoons flour
2 cups beef broth
1/2 cup sweet vermouth
1/2 cup water
Fresh rosemary sprigs for garnish

Preheat oven to 500 degrees.

In a roasting pan, thoroughly combine the onions, tomatoes, oil, and salt and pepper. Roast the mixture in the middle of a the oven for 10 minutes. Stir the mixture, put the beef, seasoned with more salt and pepper, on top of it, and bake the beef and the onion mixture for 15 minutes. Reduce the temperature to 350 degrees and roast the beef for 12 minutes more per pound, or until a meat thermometer inserted in the center of the roast registers 135 degrees, for medium-rare meat. Transfer the beef to a cutting board and let it stand for 30 minutes.

To the onion mixture, add the flour and cook over moderate heat, stirring, for 3 minutes. Whisk in the broth, vermouth, and water. Simmer the gravy, whisking and scraping up the brown bits, for 10 to 15 minutes. Let stand; skim any fat from the top. Reheat.

Carve the roast beef just before serving. Serve with gravy on the side.

# Celeried Mashed Potatoes

3 pounds russet (baking) potatoes, scrubbed
4 tablespoons unsalted butter
5 cups chopped celery, including the
   leaves (about 1/2 bunch)
1 clove garlic, pressed
1 cup milk, scalded
Salt and pepper to taste

Preheat oven to 375 degrees. Prick the potatoes a few times with a fork and bake them for 1 hour.

In a large skillet, melt the butter. Add the celery and garlic; cook covered for 10 minutes. Uncover and cook for 10 minutes, stirring frequently, until celery is tender.

Transfer mixture to a food processor and purée it. Peel the baked potatoes and mash them. Stir in the celery purée, salt and pepper, and enough milk to reach the desired consistency. Serve hot.

# Broccoli with Hazelnuts

1 onion, peeled and chopped
1 cup toasted, chopped hazelnuts
3 tablespoons butter
2 heads fresh broccoli or 2 packages
   (10 ounces each) frozen chopped
   broccoli
Salt and pepper to taste

Sauté the onion and hazelnuts in the butter until the onion is translucent.

Add the broccoli. Cover and cook on low heat until the broccoli is tender. Add a small amount of water during cooking, if necessary, to keep the vegetables from sticking to the pan. Add salt and pepper and stir gently.

# CHOCOLATE BUTTERSCOTCH PIE

Pastry for a single crust pie
2 ounces unsweetened chocolate,
   chopped
2 cups firmly packed light brown sugar
1/2 cup (1 stick) unsalted butter, at room
   temperature
3 large eggs
1/2 cup whipping cream
1 cup chilled whipping cream
1 tablespoon confectioners' sugar
Grated semisweet chocolate

Preheat oven to 400 degrees.

Line 9-inch glass pie dish with the crust. Crimp edges. Butter a large piece of foil. Place foil, buttered-side down, in crust. Bake 10 minutes. Remove foil and bake for 5 minutes more, piercing crust with a fork if bubbles appear. Cool completely.

Reduce oven temperature to 350 degrees. Melt unsweetened chocolate in top of a double boiler over simmering water, stirring until chocolate is smooth. Cool. Using an electric mixer, beat brown sugar and butter in a medium bowl until blended. Add the eggs, one at a time, beating well after each addition. Stir in 1/2 cup cream and melted chocolate.

Pour filling into prepared pie crust. Bake until filling is set, about 45 minutes. Cool pie completely. This stage can be prepared 2 hours ahead.

In a large bowl, beat the 1 cup chilled cream and confectioners' sugar to stiff peaks. Spread cream over pie. Sprinkle with grated chocolate and serve.

# SOUTHERN CHRISTMAS DINNER

### (FOR EIGHT)

*Lobster Bisque ~ Corn Bread Croutons*
*Ham with Mustard-Apple Glaze*
*Apple and Pear Chutney*
*Potato–Celery Root Purée*
*Gingered Carrots ~ Green Beans with Red Bell Pepper*
*Sweet Potato Biscuits*
*Cinnamon Chocolate Pie with Whipped Cream*
*Coffee ~ Tea*

## We suggest
- *With the bisque—a creamy, barrel-fermented chardonnay*
- *With the main course—a light Dolcetto or richer Barbaresco*
- *With dessert—a fruity muscat.*

# LOBSTER BISQUE

2 teaspoons minced onion
3 tablespoons butter
3 tablespoons flour
2 tablespoons tomato paste
3 cups hot chicken broth
2 cups minced, cooked lobster meat
1 cup milk
2 cups whipping cream
Salt and cayenne to taste

Sauté the onion in the butter until tender. Add the flour and tomato paste. Stir until completely blended. Add broth. Cook until slightly thickened, stirring all the time. Add lobster meat.

Cook over low heat for 10 minutes. Stir in milk and cream. Continue heating mixture. Do not let boil. Season with salt and cayenne before serving. Serve bisque with corn bread croutons (recipe follows).

# CORN BREAD CROUTONS

1 tablespoon olive oil
1 corn muffin, cut into 1/3-inch cubes
Salt and pepper to taste

In a skillet (preferably nonstick) heat oil over moderately high heat until hot. Sauté corn muffin cubes until golden brown and crisp. Season croutons with salt and pepper to taste. Croutons may be made one day ahead and kept in a sealed plastic bag. Reheat in the oven before serving.

# HAM WITH MUSTARD-APPLE GLAZE

1 shankless, skinless smoke-cured ham,
    12 to 14 pounds
Whole cloves for studding ham
1/2 cup apple jelly
2 tablespoons Dijon mustard

Preheat oven to 350 degrees.

Score top of ham into diamonds and stud center of each diamond with a clove. Bake ham in a roasting pan in the middle of the oven for 1 1/2 hours.

In a small saucepan heat jelly over moderate heat, stirring constantly, until melted and smooth. Remove saucepan from heat and stir in mustard. Spread glaze evenly on top of the baked ham and bake 35 minutes more.

Let the ham stand 15 minutes before carving it for the table.

# APPLE AND PEAR CHUTNEY

1 firm ripe red pear
3 tart apples
1 cup golden raisins
1/4 cup rice wine vinegar
1/4 cup sugar
1 tablespoon peeled, finely chopped fresh
    ginger
1 teaspoon mustard seeds
1/4 teaspoon ground cinnamon
1/4 teaspoon ground nutmeg

Halve and core pear and apples. Chop pear and apples into medium-size pieces.

In a saucepan combine pear and apples with remaining ingredients and bring to a simmer, stirring gently. Simmer chutney, covered, stirring occasionally, until fruit is tender, 10 to 15 minutes. Let cool. Serve chilled. Chutney may be made ahead and refrigerated.

# POTATO–CELERY ROOT PURÉE

3 large russet potatoes, peeled and cut
  into 2-inch pieces
Water to cover
1 medium celeryroot (or celeriac), peeled
  and cut into small pieces
1/2 cup half and half
1/4 cup butter
2 tablespoons finely grated orange rind
Salt and black pepper to taste

Place the potatoes and celery root in a
saucepan with enough water to cover. Bring
to a boil, reduce to simmer, and cook until
tender.

Heat the cream and the butter in a small
saucepan until the butter is melted. Drain the
potatoes and celery root. Mash the potatoes
and celery root. Quickly fold in the hot cream
mixture and the orange rind. Season with salt
and pepper.

# GINGERED CARROTS

3 pounds carrots, cut into 3- by 1/2-inch
  sticks
Water to cover
3 tablespoons light brown sugar
3 tablespoons butter
1 tablespoon peeled, finely chopped fresh
  ginger
Salt and pepper to taste

Cover carrots with water and boil, uncovered,
until tender, about 10 minutes.

While carrots are cooking, in a small
saucepan cook brown sugar, butter, and ginger over moderate heat, stirring, until butter
is melted.

Drain carrots well and toss them in a bowl
with the brown sugar glaze and salt and pepper to taste.

# Green Beans with Red Bell Pepper

2 pounds green beans, trimmed
Water to cover
4 tablespoons butter
1 red bell pepper, cut into julienne strips
Salt to taste

Cook the beans in water to cover for 3 minutes. Drain. Plunge the beans into a bowl of ice and cold water to stop the cooking. Let the beans cool completely and drain well. The beans may be prepared a day in advance if kept covered and refrigerated.

In a skillet, heat the butter over moderately high heat. Add the beans and the bell pepper, stirring, for 2 minutes or until the vegetables are crisp-tender. Season with salt.

# Sweet Potato Biscuits

1 can (1 pound) mashed sweet potatoes
2 1/4 cups buttermilk biscuit mix
1/2 cup brown sugar
1 teaspoon ground cinnamon
1/2 teaspoon ground ginger
1/2 teaspoon ground nutmeg
3 tablespoons water

Preheat oven to 350 degrees. Grease a large baking sheet. Put mashed sweet potatoes in a bowl. Stir in buttermilk biscuit mix, sugar, and spices. Add enough water, by tablespoons, to form a soft dough.

Turn out the dough onto a lightly floured surface. Pat the dough 1/2-inch thick. Cut out the biscuits using a small round biscuit or cookie cutter. Transfer biscuits to the prepared baking sheet, spacing them evenly. Bake until golden brown, about 18 minutes (biscuits will rise only slightly). Serve hot.

# CINNAMON CHOCOLATE PIE

*Filling:*
1 cup light corn syrup
1/2 cup sugar
1/4 cup margarine or butter, melted
1 teaspoon vanilla extract
1 teaspoon ground cinnamon
3 eggs
1 (6-ounce) package (1 cup) semisweet
   chocolate chips
1 1/2 cups pecan halves
Pastry for a single crust pie

*Topping:*
Whipped cream
1/2 teaspoon ground cinnamon
1 teaspoon confectioners' sugar

Heat oven to 325 degrees.

In a large bowl, combine corn syrup, sugar, margarine, vanilla, cinnamon, and eggs and beat well. Stir in the chocolate chips and pecans.

Spread the mixture evenly in a pie crust–lined pan. Bake for 55 to 65 minutes or until the filling is set. Cover edge of pie crust with strip of foil after 15 to 20 minutes of baking to prevent excessive browning. Cool completely.

Garnish pie with whipped cream to which you have added the cinnamon and powdered sugar. Keep pie refrigerated until serving time.

# Roast Goose Christmas Dinner

## (For Eight)

*Pumpkin Soup*
*Roast Goose with Port Giblet Gravy*
*Apple-Sage Dressing ~ Nutmeg Mashed Potatoes*
*Glazed Carrots and Parsnips ~ Spiced Red Cabbage*
*Apple and Mince Tart*
*Coffee ~ Tea*

### We suggest
- *With the soup—a sauvignon blanc or dry Johannisberg Riesling.*
- *With the goose—a spicy red zinfandel.*
- *Following dessert—a good Cognac or Alambic brandy.*

# Pumpkin Soup

4 tablespoons unsalted butter
1/4 cup finely chopped green onions
3 large white potatoes, peeled and cut in cubes
4 cups chicken broth, divided
1 can (1 pound 13 ounces) pumpkin, mashed
2 cups whipping cream
1/4 cup sherry
Salt and pepper
Grated nutmeg

In a deep soup pot, melt butter over medium-low heat. Add green onions and cook, stirring until transparent and wilted; do not brown. Add cubed potatoes and 1 cup of the chicken broth. Cover and simmer until tender; remove from heat.

Pour into a blender and purée. Return to the soup pot and add remaining chicken broth, pumpkin, heavy cream, and sherry. Stir and return to heat. Add salt and pepper to taste. Serve with a sprinkle of nutmeg on top of each bowl.

# ROAST GOOSE WITH PORT GIBLET GRAVY

**1 whole goose, 12 to 14 pounds**
**3 cups water**
**1 medium onion, peeled and sliced**
**1 large carrot**
**1 celery stalk, including leaves**
**Salt to taste**
**5 to 6 whole peppercorns**
**1 or 2 lemons, halved**
**Salt and pepper to taste**
**Fresh rosemary and parsley sprigs**
**2 cups boiling water**
**1 tablespoon butter**
**3 tablespoons flour**
**1 cup port (we suggest tawny port)**

Remove neck and giblets from goose, and set aside liver. Place giblets in medium saucepan with water, onion, carrot, celery, salt to taste, and peppercorns. Bring to boil, then reduce heat and simmer 1 1/2 hours, or until giblets are tender. Drain. Discard the vegetables and peppercorns. Chop the giblets. Retain the broth.

Preheat oven to 350 degrees. Remove all the excess fat from goose. Rinse and pat it dry. Rub inside and out with lemon halves and sprinkle cavity with salt to taste. Place rosemary and parsley in cavity.

Truss goose and skewer opening. Place breastside up on rack in large roasting pan. Prick the skin in several places.

Baste several times during the roasting period with boiling water. This will help get rid of the fat. Roast goose 3 hours or until meat thermometer reaches 185 degrees and thigh meat feels soft and joint moves easily, about 16 to 20 minutes per pound. As goose cooks, remove rendered fat with bulb baster and set aside. When goose is done, transfer to a warm platter and let stand 15 minutes.

Cut the liver into 4 pieces and sauté in a small amount of butter until browned on outside but still pink within. Chop for use in gravy.

Skim fat from roasting pan, add giblet stock and bring to boil over direct heat, scraping to remove browned bits from bottom of pan. Mix the rest of the butter and flour together to form a paste and add to stock. Season to taste with salt and pepper. Add port and stir in chopped giblets and liver. Simmer until gravy thickens.

# Apple-Sage Dressing

7 tablespoons butter
1 cup chopped onion
1/2 cup chopped celery
6 to 8 cups cubed bread
2 cups peeled, cored, and diced tart apple
1 cup chopped walnuts
1/4 cup chopped fresh parsley
2 eggs, beaten
2 teaspoons ground dried sage
1/2 teaspoon dried thyme
Salt and pepper to taste

Preheat oven to 350 degrees. Melt butter in a skillet. Add onion and celery and sauté until softened. Transfer to a large bowl and mix in the bread. Stir in the remaining ingredients and blend well. Place in buttered baking dish. Cover tightly with foil.

Bake 30 minutes covered. Then remove foil and bake an additional 20 minutes until top browns and begins to crisp.

# Nutmeg Mashed Potatoes

10 medium baking potatoes
Water to cover
6 tablespoons butter or margarine
2/3 cup half and half
Salt and pepper to taste
Ground nutmeg to taste
Sliced green onions for garnish

Peel potatoes and cut into quarters. Cover with water and boil for about 30 minutes or until tender. Drain well and put through a food mill or ricer, or mash with potato masher; do not use a food processor.

With an electric mixer or a whisk, whip mashed potatoes, gradually adding butter and warm cream. Season to taste with salt, pepper and nutmeg. Garnish with sliced green onions.

# GLAZED CARROTS AND PARSNIPS

1 1/2 pounds medium carrots
1 1/2 pounds medium parsnips
3/4 stick butter or margarine
1/3 cup light brown sugar
Salt to taste

Peel and cut the carrots and parsnips in half lengthwise. Heat 1 inch of water to boil in a 12-inch skillet. Add vegetables and return to boil. Reduce heat to low; cover and simmer 10 to 15 minutes until vegetables are almost tender; drain off water.

Add butter and brown sugar to carrots and parsnips in skillet. Cook over medium-high heat, gently turning vegetables occasionally, until sugar dissolves and vegetables are glazed and golden, about 10 minutes. Season with salt to taste.

# SPICED RED CABBAGE

1 medium red cabbage, shredded
Water to cover
2 tablespoons vegetable oil
1/2 cup chopped onion
2 tart apples, quartered, seeds removed, and chopped
4 tablespoons red wine vinegar
2 tablespoons sugar
1 bay leaf
Salt and pepper to taste
1/8 teaspoon ground cloves

Cover cabbage water and boil for 1 minute. Drain. Return to the kettle and stir in remaining ingredients.

Cover and simmer for 1 hour or until cabbage is tender. Remove bay leaf.

# APPLE AND MINCE TART

3 large cooking apples
Juice of 1 lemon
1 1/2 cups prepared mincemeat
2 tablespoons sugar
Ground cinnamon
Ground nutmeg
2 teaspoons butter
1/2 cup apricot preserves (optional)
Pastry for a single crust pie

Preheat oven to 375 degrees.

Peel and core 3 large, tart cooking apples. Cut in thin slices and toss with lemon juice. Spread the mincemeat in the unbaked pie shell. Top with 2 layers of overlapping apple slices. Sprinkle each layer with 1 tablespoon sugar, and ground cinnamon and nutmeg to taste; dot with butter.

Bake tart 55 to 60 minutes, until crust is golden and apples are tender. Remove from oven and, if using, glaze with 1/2 cup melted and strained apricot preserves. This is good with vanilla ice cream.

# SOUTHWEST CHRISTMAS DINNER
## (FOR EIGHT)

*Cool Cucumber Soup*
*Jicama-Orange Salad*
*Turkey Southwest Style ~ Chili Gravy*
*Mashed Potatoes ~ Acorn Squash with Sausage*
*Peppery Succotash*
*Bourbon Pecan Pie*
*Coffee ~ Tea*

## We suggest

- *With soup and salad—a grassy sauvignon blanc.*
- *With the main course—a vin gris or other dry rosé, or a light, smoky pinot noir.*

# Cool Cucumber Soup

4 medium cucumbers
2 1/2 cups buttermilk, divided
Salt and pepper to taste
2 teaspoons minced onion

Cut 4 to 8 thin slices off one cucumber and reserve for garnish. Pare all the remaining cucumber and cut it into 3/4-inch slices.

Pour 1/4 cup of the buttermilk into the blender container; add half the cucumber slices and blend on high speed until smooth. Add remaining slices, salt, pepper, and onion. Blend until smooth, about 1 minute. Stir in remaining buttermilk. Chill. Serve in cups and garnish each with a reserved cucumber slice.

This soup may be made a day or two in advance and refrigerated.

# Jicama-Orange Salad

2 medium oranges, peeled, white membrane removed, then thinly sliced
3/4 pound jicama, peeled and cut into 1/4-inch julienne sticks (about 4 cups)
1/4 cup fresh orange juice
2 tablespoons fresh lime juice
1 to 2 tablespoons fresh cilantro leaves
2 teaspoons Dijon mustard
2 teaspoons finely chopped red onion
2 tablespoons white vinegar
1/3 cup vegetable oil
1 head butter lettuce

Combine oranges and jicama. Mix orange juice with lime juice and pour over the salad; then sprinkle with the cilantro. Whisk together dressing ingredients. Serve the salad on top of lettuce leaves with the dressing on the side.

# TURKEY
# SOUTHWEST STYLE

1 whole turkey, 12 to 14 pounds
1 cup chopped onion
3/4 cup chopped celery
1/2 cup butter, divided
3 cups packaged corn bread stuffing mix
1 cup chicken broth
1 cup corn (fresh, frozen, or canned)
1/2 can (4 ounces) diced green chilies
1/2 cup chopped toasted walnuts
1 egg, lightly beaten
Dried sage to taste
Salt and pepper to taste

Preheat oven to 325 degrees. Rinse turkey, pat dry. Sauté onion and celery in 1/2 of the butter until soft. Combine the remaining ingredients except for the butter. Mix, spoon into turkey cavity, and truss. Melt the remaining butter with a bit of dried sage, and brush over the turkey.

Roast for 3 to 3 1/2 hours, until meat thermometer registers 170 degrees in breast or 180 degrees in thigh. Let stand 20 minutes before carving; reserve drippings for chili gravy.

# CHILI
# GRAVY

1/3 cup turkey fat
1/2 cup flour
4 cups chicken broth (canned or home-made) and drippings
1/2 cup diced green chilies
Dried sage to taste
Pepper to taste

Pour fat and drippings from turkey pan into 4-cup measureing cup. Skim off and reserve 1/3 cup of fat. Discard remaining fat, reserving drippings. Add chicken broth to the drippings to measure 4 cups. Melt reserved fat in saucepan; stir in 1/2 cup flour until smooth. Cook 2 minutes, stirring. Gradually add broth, chilies, sage, and a dash of pepper. Bring to a boil. Reduce heat; simmer, covered, until thickened slightly, about 5 minutes.

# MASHED POTATOES

12 medium baking potatoes
Water to cover
6 tablespoons butter or margarine
2/3 cup half and half
Salt and pepper to taste
Ground nutmeg
Sliced green onions for garnish

Peel potatoes and cut into quarters. Cover with water and boil for about 30 minutes or until tender. Drain well and put through a food mill or ricer, or mash with potato masher. Do not use a food processor.

With electric mixer or whisk, whip mashed potatoes, gradually adding butter and cream. Season to taste with salt, pepper, and nutmeg. Garnish with sliced green onions.

# ACORN SQUASH WITH SAUSAGE

4 small acorn squash
8 tablespoons maple syrup
4 tablespoons butter or margarine
1/2 pound bulk hot Italian sausage

Preheat oven to 350 degrees.

Cut squash in half; clean seeds from cavities. Put some maple syrup, butter, and sausage into each squash cavity. Place on a baking sheet. Bake for 30 to 40 minutes or until squash is fork-tender.

# PEPPERY SUCCOTASH

2 to 3 tablespoons butter or margarine
1 green bell pepper, seeded and diced
1 red bell pepper, seeded and diced
3/4 cup thinly sliced green onions, divided
2 packages (10 ounces each) frozen
    succotash
1 cup water
Salt and pepper to taste

Melt the butter in a saucepan. Add the diced peppers and 1/2 cup of the green onions; sauté 2 minutes. Add succotash and water; bring to a boil. Cover, reduce heat to medium-low, and simmer 5 to 7 minutes until succotash is tender.

Sprinkle remaining green onions over succotash; season with salt and pepper to taste. If needed, cook uncovered over medium-high heat for 1 to 2 minutes to reduce liquid, stirring often.

# BOURBON PECAN PIE

1 cup light or dark corn syrup
1/2 cup sugar
4 tablespoons butter or margarine, melted
3 lightly beaten eggs
1 to 2 tablespoons bourbon
2 cups pecan halves
Pastry for a single crust pie
Whipped cream (optional)

Preheat oven to 400 degrees.

In a mixing bowl, combine corn syrup, sugar, and melted butter. Stir in eggs, bourbon, and pecan halves. Pour mixture into unbaked pie shell. Bake 15 minutes; reduce oven temperature to 350 degrees and bake about 30 minutes longer.

Serve with lightly sweetened whipped cream, if you wish.

# Traditional Chanukah Celebration

### (For Eight)

*Borscht ~ Coleslaw ~ Tzimmes*
*Potato Latkes ~ Applesauce ~ Sour Cream*
*Sweet Potatoes ~ Carrots*
*Apple Strudel*
*A Bowl of Nuts ~ Chocolate Coins ~ A Bowl of Fruit*
*Coffee ~ Tea*

## We suggest
- *With the main course—an off-dry Riesling or a Gringnolino. If a drier red is desired, try a light merlot.*
- *With the strudel—an apple or pear brandy will complement the fruit.*

# BORSCHT

1 tablespoon vegetable oil
3 medium onions, peeled and sliced
3 bunches beets, peeled and sliced
4 vegetable bouillon cubes
3 quarts water
3 to 4 large carrots, coarsely shredded
6 medium potatoes
1/4 cup lemon juice
3 tablespoons sugar
Salt to taste

Heat oil in a large saucepan. Add onions, and sauté about 10 minutes. Add beets, bouillon cubes, and water, heat to boiling, then simmer for 30 minutes. Add carrots; simmer for 15 minutes or until carrots are tender. Cover, cool, and refrigerate.

In a smaller pan, cover potatoes with water, and boil for 30 minutes until potatoes are tender. Drain, cool, peel, and dice into 1/4-inch squares. Refrigerate.

When ready to serve, add lemon juice, sugar, and salt to borscht. Heat, and pour over 7 or 8 potato cubes in each soup bowl.

# COLESLAW

1 medium head of green cabbage
1 medium head of red cabbage
1 medium red onion, peeled
1/2 cup mayonnaise
1/4 cup cider vinegar
1/2 teaspoon sugar
3 tablespoons Dijon mustard
Salt and pepper to taste

Quarter both cabbages, remove tough ribs, and cut into thin slices. Cut onion in half lengthwise, cut into thin slices, and then cut in half. Combine onions and cabbage.

In a separate bowl, mix mayonnaise, vinegar, sugar, mustard, salt, and pepper. Add to cabbage mixture; mix well. Refrigerate until ready to serve.

# TZIMMES (BRISKET OF BEEF)

4 pounds lean brisket of beef
Salt and pepper to taste
2 medium yellow onions, peeled and
  coarsely chopped
1/2 cup celery, chopped
1/4 cup packed fresh parsley
3 cups beef broth
Juice of 1 lemon
3 to 4 whole cloves
1/2 teaspoon ground cinnamon
3 pounds sweet potatoes, peeled and
  quartered
6 medium carrots, peeled and cut into
  2-inch pieces
12 ounces pitted prunes
1 tablespoon honey
2 tablespoons white vinegar

Preheat oven to 475 degrees.

Lightly salt and pepper the brisket of beef and place meat on a rack in a large roasting pan. Brown the meat, fatty side up, in the oven for 30 minutes. Remove the meat and the rack, set aside. Add the onions, celery, and parsley to the roasting pan. Place the brisket of beef on top of the vegetables, without the rack. Add the beef broth, lemon juice, cloves, and cinnamon, and cover pan.

Reduce oven temperature to 300 degrees, and bake the brisket for 2 1/2 hours. Remove the pan from the oven, and add sweet potatoes, carrots, and the prunes. Mix honey with the vinegar and pour over meat; return the covered pan to oven and bake for 1 hour more. Slice the meat and serve with the vegetables and sauce from the pan.

# Potato Latkes

2 pounds potatoes
1 pound parsnips
2 green onions, chopped
1/4 cup flour
Salt and pepper to taste
2 large eggs, beaten
4 tablespoons vegetable oil

Peel and finely shred the potatoes and parsnips. Squeeze as much water from them as is possible. Add green onions, flour, salt, pepper, and eggs to mixture; combine thoroughly.

Heat oil in a skillet over medium heat. Drop 1/4 cup of the mixture into skillet and flatten to 3 or 4 inches in diameter. Brown on each side about 5 minutes. Place on wire rack. Repeat.

# Applesauce

2 pounds tart cooking apples
1 cup water
1 cup sugar
1/4 pound green, seedless grapes
1/2 teaspoon ground cinnamon

Peel, core, and quarter apples, removing seeds. Place in a saucepan. Add water and simmer, covered, for 8 to 10 minutes, stirring often. Add sugar, mixing thoroughly.

Remove apples from the pan and place in a food processor. Pulse, using on-off cycle for 3 or 4 seconds. Return to pan and add grapes. Bring to a boil, adding water if necessary. Remove, cool, and store in refrigerator. Sprinkle with cinnanmon before serving.

# Apple Strudel

1 cup flour
1/2 teaspoon salt
1 egg, slightly beaten
2 tablespoons vegetable oil
4 tablespoons warm water
3 tablespoons seedless raisins
3 tablespoons currants
2/3 cup confectioners' sugar
1/2 teaspoon ground cinnamon
2 pounds cooking apples, peeled, cored, and coarsely grated
3 tablespoons butter, melted
1/4 pound ground almonds
Confectioners' sugar

Lightly oil a baking sheet. Combine flour and salt in a large bowl. Make a well in the center and pour in the egg and oil.

Add the water slowly, stirring with a fork, to make a soft, sticky dough. Work the dough in the bowl until it leaves the sides of the bowl. Then place on a lightly floured surface and gently knead for 12 to 15 minutes.

Form the dough into a ball, place it on a cloth, and cover the dough with a warmed bowl. Let it rest in a warm place for an hour. Put the raisins, currants, sugar, cinnamon, and apples into a bowl and mix very thoroughly.

With a warm rolling pin, roll the dough on a clean, lightly floured suface to a 1/8-inch thickness, turning and lifting to prevent it from sticking.

Gently stretch the dough on all sides until it is paper thin, then trim to about 24 inches by 27 inches. Let it rest for about 15 minutes.

Preheat oven to 375 degrees. Place the dough with one of the long sides toward you; brush with melted butter and sprinkle with ground almonds.

Spread the apple mixture evenly over the dough, leaving a 2-inch border all around. Fold the border in over the apple mixture.

Gently lift the corners of the dough nearest to you and begin to roll up the strudel. Stop after each turn and pat it into shape. Slide it onto the prepared baking sheet, and brush with melted butter.

Bake for about 40 minutes until golden brown. Decorate with confectioners' sugar. Slice, and serve hot or cold.

# Elegant New Year's Dinner

## (For Six)

Sherried Carrot Soup
Hearts of Palm Salad
Cornish Game Hens with Fruit and Nut Stuffing
Sweet Potato Puff ~ Cucumber Sauté
Parker House Rolls
Butter Cookies
Coffee ~ Tea

### We suggest
- *To toast the New Year—glasses of the best champagne.*
- *With the soup—a dry sherry or vermouth.*
- *With the game hens—a good burgundy or chardonnay.*
- *With dessert and coffee—Cointreau or Grand Marnier.*

# SHERRIED CARROT SOUP

1 onion, chopped
2 tablespoons unsalted butter
6 carrots, peeled and cut into 1/4-inch-thick slices
1/4 teaspoon ground ginger
1/4 teaspoon ground cinnamon
4 1/2 cups chicken broth
1/4 cup medium-dry sherry
1 cup whipping cream

In a saucepan, fry the onion in the butter over low heat, stirring until the onion is softened. Add the carrots, ginger, and cinnamon, and cook the mixture, stirring, for 1 minute.

Add the broth and bring the mixture to a boil. Simmer, stirring occasionally, for 20 minutes, or until the carrots are very tender. In a food processor purée the mixture in batches, pouring the puréed soup into another saucepan as you go. Add the sherry and the cream. Bring the soup to a boil and simmer for 5 minutes.

# HEARTS OF PALM SALAD

2 tablespoons fresh lemon juice
2 1/2 teaspoons Dijon mustard
1 clove garlic, finely minced
6 tablespoons olive oil
Salt and pepper to taste
1 can (14 ounces) hearts of palm, drained and sliced into rounds
1 can (14 ounces) artichoke hearts, drained and quartered
1 head butter lettuce
12 cherry tomatoes, halved

Combine the lemon juice, mustard, and garlic in a bowl. Gradually whisk in olive oil. Season dressing to taste with salt and pepper. Add hearts of palm and artichoke hearts. Let marinate at room temperature at least 20 minutes and up to 4 hours, tossing occasionally.

Line six plates with lettuce leaves. Divide the hearts of palm and artichoke hearts among the plates. Garnish with tomatoes. Spoon remaining dressing over the salad, and serve.

# CORNISH GAME HENS

6 Cornish hens
Salt to taste
1 1/2 cups apricot nectar
3 tablespoons apricot jam
3 tablespoons light brown sugar
6 whole cloves
1/2 teaspoon ground cinnamon
4 tablespoons dry white wine
1 1/2 teaspoons cornstarch
Fruit and Nut Stuffing (recipe follows)

Preheat oven to 425 degrees. Wash hens; dry with absorbent paper. Salt hens inside and out and set aside. Prepare stuffing. Stuff hens. Fasten skin with skewers; tie legs securely. Place on a rack of a baking pan.

Combine nectar, jam, brown sugar, cloves, and cinnamon in a pot. Boil, stirring constantly. Combine wine and cornstarch; stir into nectar mixture. Cook until thick and smooth. Baste hens. Roast for 1 hour, basting continuously.

# FRUIT AND NUT STUFFING

2 cups fine dry bread crumbs
6 tablespoons butter, melted
1 cup coarsely chopped dried fruit
3/4 cup chopped pecans or walnuts
3/4 teaspoon dried rosemary
3/4 teaspoon dried thyme
Salt to taste

In a large bowl combine bread crumbs and melted butter. Add dried fruit, nuts, and seasonings. Mix well. Stuff.

# Sweet Potato Puff

2 cans (16 ounces each) sweet potatoes in
    light syrup, drained
3 eggs, separated
1 cup half-and-half or light cream
2 tablespoons flour
2 tablespoons brown sugar
Salt and pepper to taste
1/4 teaspoon ground nutmeg
1/4 teaspoon ground cinnamon

Preheat oven to 400 degrees. In a food processor, combine the potatoes, egg yolks, cream,
flour, brown sugar, salt, and the spices. Pulse
until mixture is smooth. In a large bowl, beat
egg whites until stiff but not dry. Gently fold
the potato mixture into the beaten egg whites.

Spoon or pour mixture into a buttered 1-
quart baking dish. Place dish in a pan of hot
water and bake 15 minutes. Reduce oven
temperature to 350 degrees and bake about
25 minutes longer or until puffed and gold-
en on top. Serve immediately.

# Cucumber Sauté

2 large cucumbers, peeled
2 tablespoons butter or margarine
2 tablespoons flour
3/4 cup half-and-half
2 tablespoons dried dill weed
1 teaspoon granulated sugar
Salt to taste
Dash white pepper

Cut peeled cucumbers in half lengthwise
and scrape out seeds with spoon. Cut cucumbers in 1/2-inch cubes. Sauté in butter in
large, heavy pan until tender but still firm,
about 2 minutes. Sprinkle with flour and stir
to blend. Add half-and-half, dill, sugar, salt,
and pepper.

Cook over moderate heat until thickened,
stirring constantly. If serving is delayed and
sauce becomes too thick, add a little more
half-and-half.

# SOUTHERN NEW YEAR'S DINNER

## (FOR EIGHT)

*Corn Chowder*
*Herbed New Year's Roast Chicken with Gravy*
*Quick Hoppin' John*
*Green Bean Almond Sauté ~ Orange Sweet Potato Casserole*
*Cranberry Mold with Grapes ~ Tomatoes with Tarragon*
*Pecan Biscuits*
*Coconut Pie with Vanilla Ice Cream*
*Coffee ~ Tea*

## We suggest
- *With the main course—a full-bodied chardonnay or pinot blanc.*
  *A Gewürztraminer would work if a sweeter wine is desired.*
- *With dessert—a muscat-based sparkling wine.*

# CORN CHOWDER

1 large white onion, peeled and diced
1 stalk celery, diced
2 carrots, peeled and diced
3 strips of smoked bacon, diced
3 tablespoons corn oil
2 cloves minced garlic
1 cup white wine
6 ears of fresh corn, kernels removed
   from the cobs, or 3 cups frozen corn,
   thawed
3 cups chicken broth
2 cups whipping cream
2 tablespoons chopped fresh thyme
2 tablespoons chopped fresh basil
Salt and pepper to taste
Tabasco to taste

Sauté onion, celery, carrots, and bacon with corn oil until soft.

Add garlic and cook approximately 1 minute. Add white wine and cook 3 minutes over medium heat. Add corn, chicken broth, cream, and thyme. Cook until tender. Add basil, salt and pepper, and Tabasco to taste. Remove half of the soup, purée in processor or blender, and add back to remainder of the soup.

# HERBED NEW YEAR'S ROAST CHICKEN WITH GRAVY

1 whole roasting chicken, 5 to 7 pounds
4 green onions
3 tablespoons butter or margarine, softened
1 tablespoon minced fresh sage leaves or 1 teaspoon dried sage
1 tablespoon minced fresh thyme leaves or 1 teaspoon dried thyme
2 tablespoons flour
2 cups chicken broth or 1 cup each chicken broth and half-and-half or light cream

Preheat oven to 350 degrees.

Remove giblets from chicken and set aside. Rinse chicken inside and out and pat dry. In food processor, combine green onions, butter, sage, and thyme. Pulse on and off several times to form a paste. Rub mixture inside and outside the chicken, placing any remaining mixture in the chicken cavity. Roast for 2 to 2 1/2 hours (15 to 20 minutes per pound), until juices run clear and there is no hint of pink when thigh is pierced. Remove chicken to serving platter and keep warm.

To prepare gravy, pour pan juices into a heatproof measuring cup. Skim off 3 tablespoons clear yellow drippings from top of juices and return to roasting pan. Discard remaining clear drippings from measuring cup, reserving degreased juices for gravy; add enough chicken broth to make 2 1/2 cups total liquid. Stir flour into roasting pan. Cook roasting pan over medium heat 4 to 5 minutes until well browned, stirring and scraping bottom of pan. Gradually stir in broth mixture; simmer 3 to 4 minutes until gravy is thickened, stirring occasionally.

# QUICK HOPPIN' JOHN

1/2 pound lean bacon
1 cup chopped onions
1 cup regular long-grain rice
1 can (16 ounces) black-eyed peas
1 2/3 cups chicken broth or water

In a large skillet, cook bacon slowly until crisp. Remove bacon, drain on paper towels, crumble, and reserve. Pour off all but 1 tablespoon bacon drippings from pan. Add onion and sauté about 5 minutes or until translucent.

Stir in rice, undrained peas, and broth. Cover and simmer 20 to 30 minutes until rice is tender. Add reserved crumbled bacon and toss to combine; serve warm.

# GREEN BEAN ALMOND SAUTÉ

2 pounds green beans
Water to cover
2 tablespoons olive oil
1/4 teaspoon pepper
1/2 cup sliced almonds

Trim ends from green beans. In a saucepan cover the green beans with water and bring to a boil. Cover and simmer 5 to 10 minutes until green beans are tender-crisp. Drain.

In the same pan, heat olive oil and add green beans, almonds, and pepper. Stir occasionally until beans are tender and they begin to brown.

# Orange Sweet Potato Casserole

3 pounds medium sweet potatoes or yams
1/3 cup half-and-half
1/4 cup (1/2 stick) butter, at room temperature,
   divided
1/2 cup orange marmalade
2 large eggs, beaten to blend
3/4 teaspoon ground allspice
1/2 teaspoon ground cinnamon
Pecans, toasted and chopped (optional)

Butter an 8-inch glass baking dish with 2-inch high sides. Place potatoes in a large saucepan; cover with water and bring to a boil. Cover and simmer until potatoes are very soft. Drain potatoes. Peel and trim.

Preheat oven to 350 degrees. Place potatoes in a food processor, add all remaining ingredients except pecans and a few teaspoons of butter. Process until mixture is smooth. The processing may have to be done in several batches. Transfer mixture to prepared baking dish. Dot mixture with remaining butter.

Bake soufflé until the center is set and the top begins to brown, about 50 minutes. Garnish with pecans if using.

# CRANBERRY MOLD WITH GRAPES

2 cups boiling water
2 packages (3 ounces each) raspberry-
flavored gelatin
2 cans (16 ounces each) whole cranberry
sauce
1 can (13 1/2 ounces) crushed pineapple
1 pound seedless green grapes, washed
and drained

Pour boiling water over the gelatin, stirring until gelatin is dissolved. Add the cranberry sauce and the pineapple with its syrup. Stir until mixed thoroughly. Pour into a 2-quart ring mold; chill until firm.

Unmold onto a large serving plate. Separate the grapes into small bunches (serving size). Place the grapes in the center of mold and around edge.

# TOMATOES WITH TARRAGON

8 large tomatoes, sliced horizontally
1/2 cup olive oil
1/2 cup balsamic vinegar
Salt and pepper to taste
1 bunch fresh tarragon, stemmed

Arrange tomatoes on platter. Drizzle the tomatoes with oil, then with vinegar. Season with salt and pepper. Sprinkle with tarragon and serve.

# PECAN BISCUITS

2 1/2 cups flour
2 tablespoons sugar
1 teaspoon grated orange peel
1/2 teaspoon baking soda
1/2 teaspoon salt
1/2 cup chilled butter, cut into pieces
1 cup pecans, toasted and chopped
1 1/4 cups buttermilk, divided

Preheat oven to 425 degrees.

Combine the flour, sugar, orange peel, baking soda, and salt in large bowl. Add butter and blend with fingertips until the mixture resembles coarse meal. Mix in the pecans and 1 cup buttermilk. Stir until the dough just forms.

Transfer dough to a floured surface and pat it to a 3/4-inch thickness. Cut into rounds, using a 2-inch-wide biscuit cutter. Transfer to an ungreased baking sheet. Brush tops of biscuits with buttermilk. Bake until golden brown, about 18 minutes.

# COCONUT PIE

1/2 cup butter
1 1/4 cups sugar
3 eggs, beaten
4 teaspoons fresh lemon juice
1 teaspoon vanilla extract
1 1/4 cups sweetened shredded coconut
Vanilla ice cream (optional)
Pastry for a single crust pie

Preheat oven to 450 degrees. Press the crust into 9-inch glass pie plate. Trim and crimp edges. Bake crust until light golden, about 9 minutes. Transfer to rack and cool. Reduce oven temperature to 350 degrees.

Melt butter in a saucepan over low heat. Add sugar and stir mixture until sugar is dissolved. Transfer to a bowl. Add eggs, lemon juice, and vanilla, and whisk to combine. Stir in the coconut.

Pour filling into the crust. Bake until the pie is deep golden brown and the custard set, about 40 minutes. Cool on a rack.

Serve with vanilla ice cream.

# SUPER BOWL BUFFET
## FOR EIGHT

*Mustard Glazed Ham*
*Boston Baked Beans*
*Green Salad with Vinaigrette Dressing*
*Assorted breads ~ Chunky Applesauce*
*Pecan Tarts*
*A Bowl of Fresh Fruit ~ A Bowl of Nuts*
*Coffee ~ Tea ~ Soft Drinks*

## We suggest
- *With the ham—a light-bodied cabernet, a Riesling, or a chenin blanc.*
- *With dessert—a sweet sherry.*

# Mustard Glazed Ham

10-pound ham, fully cooked (see note)
1 cup light brown sugar
1/4 cup maple syrup
2 tablespoons dry mustard
12 whole cloves

Remove the ham from refrigerator an hour before you are ready to bake.

Preheat the oven to 325 degrees.

Prepare the glaze by mixing the brown sugar, maple syrup, and mustard together thoroughly.

Remove the skin and most of the fat from ham, leaving about a 1/4-inch layer of fat. Place on a rack in a roasting pan. Roast for 1 hour.

Remove from the oven and score the fat in a criss-cross pattern, about 1 inch apart. Stud the cloves in the center of each square. Return ham to the oven and bake for 30 minutes. Baste the ham two or three times during the last 30 minutes of cooking.

Remove from oven; cool. Slice 6 or 7 slices and fan them out on a serving platter.

# BOSTON BAKED BEANS

2 1/2 cups Great Northern navy beans or
  small white beans
Water
1/2 pound salt pork
2 tablespoons dry mustard
1/2 cup dark brown sugar, packed
1/2 cup molasses
Salt to taste
2 1/2 cups warm water

Sort through beans, removing debris and any broken beans. Wash them and place in a large pot, covering them with enough water to come at least 3 inches above the beans.

Cover the pot, boil for 2 or 3 minutes, and turn off heat. Uncover and let beans soak for an hour.

Bring the pot to a boil again, turn heat down. Move lid slightly so that the steam can escape; simmer for 30 minutes. Drain the beans thoroughly, discarding the liquid.

Preheat oven to 325 degrees.

Score the salt pork, and cut into 4 pieces. Place 1 piece in bottom of a bean pot and cover with beans. Place 2 midway, covering each with beans, and place the last piece on the very top.

In a bowl, stir together the mustard, brown sugar, molasses, salt, and warm water. Mix thoroughly, and pour over the beans and pork. Bake for 4 hours, covered, checking frequently to see if beans are sticking to bottom of pan and require more water.

After 4 hours, remove cover and bake for an additional hour. Cool, and refrigerate for up to three days before serving. Warm for 30 minutes before serving. Adjust the seasonings.

# Green Salad with Vinaigrette Dressing

1 bunch fresh basil
1 head Belgian endive
1 head radicchio
2 bunches watercress or arugula
2 heads butter lettuce

*Vinaigrette dressing:*
1/2 cup wine vinegar
Salt to taste
1 teaspoon dry mustard
1 cup mild olive oil
2 tablespoons fresh minced tarragon
   or dill

Rinse all of the greens very thoroughly in running cold water. Remove the stems from the basil and discard them. Tear large leaves into small pieces, keep small leaves intact. Toss lightly to mix greens.

Refrigerate in a container, covered with a damp cloth until ready to serve.

Combine all ingredients for dressing very thoroughly. Store in refrigerator until ready to serve.

# Chunky Applesauce

4 delicious apples or other sweet apples
4 Granny Smith apples or other tart apples
1/4 cup brown sugar
1/2 cup cranberry juice
2 tablespoons butter
Pinch of salt
1/4 teaspoon ground cinnamon
1/4 cup raisins
2 teaspoons lemon juice

Peel, core, and quarter the apples. Place the apples, brown sugar, cranberry juice, butter, salt, and cinnamon in a large saucepan. Cover and simmer for 30 minutes. Make sure the apples don't burn by adding water if necessary.

Uncover pot, reduce heat to low. Add raisins and cook for 1 hour until sauce is thick and still chunky. Stir frequently to prevent burning.

Cool, add lemon juice and refrigerate. Serve cold or at room temperature.

# Pecan Tarts

Pastry for a single crust pie
1 egg
1/4 cup sugar
1/8 teaspoon salt
2 tablespoons butter, melted
1/3 cup corn syrup
1/2 cup pecan halves or pieces

Preheat oven to 375 degrees.

Divide dough for a single crust pie into 8 portions. Cut and form each into balls, then roll out into 4-inch circles. Gently press into muffin pans, pleating as necessary to form small pastry shells.

In a mixing bowl beat egg, sugar, salt, butter, and syrup thoroughly. Add nuts. Pour into muffin cups. Bake 35 minutes or until pastry is light brown. Cool and serve.

# Holiday Beverages

### Cold Drinks
*Claret Cup ~ Cranberry Royale*
*New Year's Ambrosia ~ Sangria Champagne*
*Sangria ~ Classic Eggnog*
*Brandy Milk Punch ~ Royal Kir ~ Holiday Punch*
*North Pole Cocktail ~ Mimosa ~ Christmas Punch*

### Hot Drinks
*Mulled Wine ~ Hot Spiced Wine*
*Hot Spiced Apple Wine ~ Swedish Glogg*
*Hot Toddy ~ Brandy Toddy with Ginger*
*Mocha Mint Café ~ The Wassail Bowl ~ Mulled Port*

## CLARET CUP

*24 servings*

1/2 cup blackberry brandy or liqueur
2 bottles dry red wine
2 tablespoons grenadine
1/2 cup Cointreau or Triple Sec
1 quart club soda
Juice of three lemons
Juice of three oranges
1 pineapple, peeled, cored, and crushed in blender
Fresh fruit slices

Combine all ingredients. Pour over a large block of ice in a punchbowl. Garnish with fresh fruit slices.

## CRANBERRY ROYALE

*6 servings*

12 tablespoons frozen cranberry juice
    concentrate, thawed
1 bottle champagne or other sparkling wine, chilled
12 whole fresh cranberries
6 orange slices, folded in half
6 bamboo skewers

Measure 2 tablespoons cranberry concentrate into each of six champagne flutes. Top with champagne. Thread 1 cranberry, 1 orange slice, and then another cranberry onto each skewer. Place skewers atop glasses.

## NEW YEAR'S AMBROSIA

*About 6 to 8 servings*

1/2 cup apple brandy
1/2 cup brandy
1/4 cup Triple Sec or Grand Marnier
1 bottle brut champagne, chilled

Shake all ingredients, except champagne, with ice. Strain into flutes and fill with champagne.

## SANGRIA CHAMPAGNE

*About 4 servings*

1/4 cup Triple Sec
1/4 cup sugar, to taste
1/2 cup grapefruit juice
Several dashes of lime juice
1 bottle brut champagne, chilled
1 lime, sliced very thin

Mix all ingredients except champagne, and chill. Pour into punchbowl or pitcher with lots of ice. Add champagne, slowly, and stir gently.

## SANGRIA

*About 4 servings*

1 bottle dry red wine
1 ounce brandy
Juice of 1 fresh orange
Juice of 1 lemon or lime
2 to 3 tablespoons sugar

6 very thin orange slices
6 very thin lemon slices
6 slices of any fresh fruit, such as peaches,
   or 15 to 20 fresh grapes.
1 bottle club soda (optional)

Mix wine, brandy, fruit juices, and sugar until well blended. Chill. Just before serving, add club soda, if using, and fruit slices. Serve from a well-chilled pitcher with lots of ice cubes.

## CLASSIC EGGNOG

*6 servings*

2 cups whipping cream
1 cup half-and-half
6 large egg yolks
1/4 cup sugar
1 teaspoon ground nutmeg
3/4 cup dry sherry
Additional ground nutmeg

Bring cream and half-and-half to a simmer in a large saucepan. Whisk yolks and sugar in a large bowl to blend. Gradually whisk hot cream mixture into yolk mixture. Return mixture to the same saucepan. Stir over medium-low heat until mixture thickens, about 4 minutes (do not boil). Strain into bowl. Stir in nutmeg. Cool slightly. (Can be made up to a week ahead. Cover and chill. If desired, rewarm over low heat, stirring occasionally.) Divide warm or cold mixture among six cups or glasses. Stir 1 tablespoon sherry into each. Sprinkle additional nutmeg over each and serve.

## BRANDY MILK PUNCH

*8 servings*

2 1/4 cups very cold milk
1 cup brandy
1/4 cup coffee liqueur
2 tablespoons vanilla extract
1/4 teaspoon (scant) ground nutmeg
10 ice cubes

Place half of each ingredient in blender. Blend on high until punch is smooth and frothy. Pour punch into four glasses. Repeat process with remaining ingredients and serve.

## ROYAL KIR

*1 serving*

3/4 cup champagne or sparkling wine
1 tablespoon crème de cassis
1 lemon twist

Pour the crème de cassis and then the champagne into a champagne flute, stir, and garnish with the lemon twist. White wine may be used in place of champagne.

## HOLIDAY PUNCH

*About 8 servings*

1 1/3 cups confectioners' sugar
1 1/3 cups of water
8 lemon peels
12 cloves

2 cinnamon sticks
6 ripe pears or peaches, peeled and diced
2 cups orange juice
1/2 cup lemon juice
2 bottles light red wine
1 lemon, sliced thinly
1 orange, sliced thinly

Combine, sugar, water, lemon peel, cloves, cinnamon sticks, and fruit in a large saucepan and bring to a boil. Simmer for 5 minutes or until the mixture becomes a light syrup. Cool and strain. Add orange juice, lemon juice and, if desired, refrigerate until ready to serve. Just before serving, add wine. Pour into pitcher or punchbowl with lots of ice.

## North Pole Cocktail

*4 servings*

4 egg whites
1/4 cup lemon juice
1/4 cup grenadine
1/2 cup dry gin
Whipped cream

Shake ingredients with ice and strain into four cocktail glasses. Top with whipped cream.

## Mimosa

*4 to 6 servings*

1 bottle brut champagne, chilled
2 cups of fresh orange juice, chilled

Mix just before serving, serve ice cold. Add one or two ice cubes to each glass, if desired.

## Christmas Punch

*20 servings*

2 cinnamon sticks
12 whole cloves
1 1/2 cups sugar
1 1/2 cups warm water
6 strips lemon peel
4 ripe pears, diced
1/2 cup lemon juice
2 cups orange juice
2 bottles medium-light red wine
1/2 cup brandy (optional)
1 finely sliced lemon
1 finely sliced orange

Combine spices, sugar, water, lemon peel, and pears in a large saucepan and bring to a boil. Simmer for 5 minutes until the mixture has become a light syrup. Cool and strain. Add lemon juice, orange juice, wine, and brandy if using. Stir thoroughly and pour over a large block of ice in a punchbowl. Garnish with the lemon and orange slices.

## Mulled Wine

*About 8 to 10 servings*

2 cups water
2 cups sugar
1 orange, thinly sliced
1 lemon, thinly sliced
2 cinnamon sticks
12 whole cloves
12 whole allspice berries
2 bottles (750 ml each) dry red wine

Combine water, sugar, orange, lemon, cinnamon sticks, cloves, and allspice berries in a large saucepan. Stir over medium heat until sugar dissolves. Increase heat and bring to boil. Reduce heat and simmer 5 minutes. Add wine and simmer 10 minutes. Strain wine into mugs. Garnish with additional cinnamon sticks and serve.

## Hot Spiced Wine

*6 servings*

1 bottle (750 ml) dry red wine or 1 bottle (25.4 ounces) nonalcoholic cabernet sauvignon wine
2 small oranges, in 1/4-inch slices
1 lemon, thinly sliced
1/2 cup fresh orange juice
6 tablespoons sugar
20 whole cloves

Combine wine, 5 orange slices, 3 lemon slices, the fresh orange juice, sugar, and 8 of the whole cloves in heavy medium saucepan. Bring to a boil. Remove from heat; cover and let stand 30 minutes. Strain. Return to same saucepan. (Can be made one day ahead. Cover; chill. Rewarm before serving.) Stud 6 orange slices with 2 cloves each. Divide orange slices and 6 lemon slices among cups. Pour spiced wine over.

## Hot Spiced Apple Wine

*About 8 to 10 servings*

6 cups fruity red wine (such as Beaujolais)
6 cups apple cider
1/4 cup sugar
1 orange, thinly sliced
1 lemon, thinly sliced
1 lime, thinly sliced
1 cinnamon stick (2 inches)
8 whole cloves
8 allspice berries
8 whole black peppercorns

Combine all ingredients in large saucepan. Bring to simmer over low heat, stirring occasionally; do not boil. Strain. Ladle punch into mugs and serve.

## SWEDISH GLOGG

*8 servings*

2 bottles dry red wine
1/2 cup superfine sugar
2 cinnamon sticks
8 whole cloves
1/4 to 1/2 cup Cognac or brandy
1/4 cup raisins
1/4 cup slivered almonds
Additional 8 cinnamon sticks for garnish (optional)

Warm all ingredients, except raisins and almonds, almost to boiling, but do not boil. In mugs or cups place a few raisins and a few almonds and add hot liquids. Garnish with cinnamon sticks, if using.

## HOT TODDY

*1 serving*

1/4 cup brandy
1 tablespoon sugar
4 whole cloves
1/2 teaspoon ground cinnamon
Slice of lemon
Boiling water
1/2 teaspoon grated nutmeg
Cinnamon stick

Warm a coffee mug, and add all ingredients, except nutmeg, and fill with boiling water. Stir to dissolve sugar, and top with nutmeg. Add cinnamon stick, and serve.

## BRANDY TODDY WITH GINGER

*4 servings*

1/4 cup firmly packed light brown sugar
3 cups water
3-inch piece of fresh ginger, sliced very
    thin crosswise
3 tablespoons fresh lemon juice
Lemon slices for garnish (optional)
3/4 cup brandy

In a saucepan combine the sugar, water, ginger, and lemon juice to taste. Simmer, covered, stirring occasionally, for 15 minutes. Discard the ginger with a slotted spoon and stir in the brandy to taste. Divide the toddy among four heated mugs and garnish each drink with a lemon slice if using.

## MOCHA MINT CAFÉ

*4 to 6 servings*

1/4 cup crème de cacao
1/4 cup crème de menthe
1/4 cup brandy
Good, fresh black coffee
Whipped cream (optional)

Blend crème de cacao, crème de menthe, and brandy, and pour into mugs or tall glasses. Fill each with coffee. Top with whipped cream.

## THE WASSAIL BOWL

*12 servings*

1/4 teaspoon ground cardamom
2 cinnamon sticks
3 whole cloves
1/4 teaspoon ground ginger
1/4 teaspoon ground nutmeg
1 cup water
1/2 cup brandy
2 bottles medium dry sherry
1 cup sugar
4 egg yolks
6 egg whites
6 medium baked apples

In a large saucepan, simmer the spices in water for 10 minutes. Add the brandy, sherry, and sugar and heat but do not boil. Combine the egg yolks with one cup of the sherry mixture, and pour into a punch bowl. Gradually add the remaining sherry mixture. Beat in the egg whites until they are frothy. Garnish with the baked apples. Serve warm.

## MULLED PORT

*6 servings*

2 oranges, peeled and thinly sliced
  (reserve the peel)
1 cinnamon stick
12 whole cloves
1/2 teaspoon ground mace
1/2 teaspoon ground nutmeg
1/2 teaspoon ground allspice
1/4 cup sugar
1 bottle ruby or tawny port

In a large nonaluminum saucepan, place the orange peel, cinnamon, cloves, mace, nutmeg, allspice, sugar, and 2 cups of water. Use medium heat, and stir to dissolve sugar. Let the mixture come to a boil, then turn down and simmer for 10 minutes. Strain, and return to pan. Add port, but do not boil. Serve in Irish coffee glasses or mugs, with a slice of the peeled orange in each0.

# INDEX OF RECIPES

Sweet Potato Puff...58
Tomatoes with Tarragon...64

## SAUCES AND RELISHES

Apple and Pear Chutney...35
Applesauce...53
Chunky Applesauce...70
Cranberry Relish with Pears and
    Apples...19
Cranberry Sauce...9
Cranberry–Ginger Chutney...26

## DESSERTS

Apple and Mince Tart...44
Apple Strudel...54
Bourbon Pecan Pie...49
Chocolate Butterscotch Pie...32
Cinnamon Chocolate Pie...38
Classic New England Cider
    Pie...20
Coconut Pie...65
Mincemeat Pie...12
Pecan Tarts...70
Pumpkin Pie...12, 27

## BEVERAGES

Brandy Milk Punch...73
Brandy Toddy with Ginger...76
Christmas Punch...74
Claret Cup...72
Classic Eggnog...73
Cranberry Royale...72

Holiday Punch...73
Hot Spiced Apple Wine...75
Hot Spiced Wine...75
Hot Toddy...76
Mimosa...74
Mocha Mint Café...76
Mulled Port...77
Mulled Wine...75
New Year's Ambrosia...72
North Pole Cocktail...74
Royal Kir...73
Sangria Champagne...72
Sangria...72
Swedish Glogg...76
The Wassail Bowl...77

The Crossing Press
publishes a full selection of cookbooks.
To receive our current catalog,
please call toll-free,
800-777-1048.